WICKED WIT

Wicked Wit

poems

PUBLIC POETRY

Public Poetry Press

TAKING POETRY PUBLIC

Poems Judged by: Diannely Antigua, John Gorman, Jason Koo

ISBN 978-1-0879-2214-0

Cover Artwork: Lydia Bodnar-Balahutrak
Book Design: Fran Sanders and Yolanda Movsessian
Proofreader: Leila Merrill

FUNDED IN PART BY
THE CITY OF HOUSTON
THROUGH HOUSTON ARTS ALLIANCE

Texas
Commission
on the Arts

TABLE OF CONTENTS

ABOUT THE COVER

Mister Bubbles (from *Boxed* series, 2010)
acrylic plastic, metal, wood and battery light, in a box frame
9 x 7 x 3 inches

I've always been fascinated with the power and metaphoric potential of words — their multiple meanings and their ability to conjure up images or a story. *Mister Bubbles* is part of a series of mixed media reliefs that are intended as visual plays on words or phrases.

The *Boxed* series is a group of playful concrete manifestations of the verbal. From within diminutive stages, miniature sculpted figures whimsically play out the words.

The figures are found or hand-sculpted forms, often gessoed and painted in grisaille. Along with an assortment of mini-props and backdrops of fragments of all kinds, they jut out from their framed "stages" and enact a visual "drama."

By association, *Mister Bubbles* presents a deceptive appearance of strength in the context of a weightlifting macho man wearing a formidable mask of a horned bull. This pseudo strongman hides behind the bull's head in order to intimidate and overpower, a bullheaded bully. However, his body is flaccid and bulbously round, a laughable empty plastic shell with air bubbles in his groin, and no guts. *Mister Bubbles* is obviously full of hot air, with bubbles that can easily be popped.

Although the series dates from ten years ago, it's almost uncanny how my work speaks to 2020. Now, due to the pandemic we're all finding ourselves "boxed" in, one way or another, and in our own personal bubbles. I've discovered that this art work exhibits its own "Wicked Wit"! Enjoy!

Lydia Bodnar-Balahutrak

Lydia Bodnar-Balahutrak completed her undergraduate art studies at Kent State University, studied at the Corcoran School of Art and received her Master of Fine Arts degree in painting from George Washington University in Washington, D.C. Born and raised in Cleveland, Ohio, she moved to Houston in 1977, where she continues to live and work.

A Fulbright IREX grant enabled her to travel to Ukraine for the first time in 1991; five years later she visited the Chernobyl Zone. These trips marked turning points in her creative work and world view. A concern with the human condition – always at the heart of her art – took new form and urgency. Her current work continues to explore narrative and cultural metaphor by combining collage, text, and figuration.

Since 1991, the artist has participated in several national and international exhibitions and been awarded artist residencies in France, Ukraine, and U.S. venues. Her work can be found in museum and private collections in the USA and Europe, including The Museum of South Texas and Oxford University. A monograph focusing on her art from 1979-2001 was published in 2005. In spring 2021, a year-long travelling solo exhibition of her work opens at the National Museum in Lviv, Ukraine, and continues to art venues in Chernivtsi, Lutsk, Kyiv, and Kharkiv.

Lydia Bodnar-Balahutrak is on the Studio School Faculty of the Glassell School of Art, Museum of Fine Arts, Houston.

http://www.lydiabodnarbalahutrak.com

INTRODUCTION

WICKED WIT could be an anthem for 2020. A virus going viral that requires more than a measure of humor to get through. A novel twist of fate that wrings wry irony out of everyday incidents. Inside our bubbles, we're all working with the remnants of how things were and still finding ways to make us laugh.

While living virtually continues to expand into most of our lives, having a book to hold, to thumb through pages, to underline and write in the margins is a comforting pleasure. We experience a connection and continuity. Books create calm and elicit simple familiar recollections....we're turning on the light next to a comfy chair, looking at our shelves and lingering there, pulling one out of the stack piled on the floor, settling in on a rainy day, picking up an old favorite resting on the bedside table, making a drink to fit the occasion and pausing to reflect. Now, it's something we can still savor.

The poems in this anthology were culled from among more than 350 submissions nationwide that were sent to Public Poetry. The final selection was made by Dianelly Antigua, Jason Koo and John Gorman.

Current slang turns "wicked" on its head to mean the opposite: "very good" or "showing great skill". These are some wicked poems, for sure. By another definition, if you describe someone or something as wicked, you can also mean that they are bad, but in a way that you find enjoyable. Enjoy it!

Fran Sanders
October 2020

PUBLIC POETRY PRIZE WINNER

Alice Friman: Shopping with Descartes

Like a supermarket chicken,
a brain weighs about three pounds,
without feathers of course.
Thoughts, like feathers, weigh
next to nothing—whimsies
of no matter. What's a thought?
A twitch, a little quiver in the jelly
quickened to life by a shock
of electricity before slipping
back into the fold it was born in.

Still, thoughts are important.
If I don't come up with a thought
for three days, my brain morphs
into a daisy stuck in the vase
of my neck. After two weeks
I could generate a bouquet.

People who think about thoughts
are philosophers. People who
think about thinking about
thoughts are epistemologists.
The book says God once had
a thought which he tucked inside
a word, which makes God a linguist.
It must have been a big word—

an abracadabra word, powerful enough
to create the sun, moon, earth, lions,
tigers, birds and bugs. Imagine,

all in six days. On the seventh day
he rested—so tired from repeating
his word he had to go to bed without
another thought in his head. And that's
when we got the flowers.

SECOND PLACE

Elina Petrova: **Pencil**

Sorry, I stole a pencil from the Shepherd School
to write this poem. Blessed are the bipolar
for they know which phase they face.
I shed silent tears and smile as I walk
Rice University trails. See, there is clover,
several drops of wild strawberries
for those who bow to grass. Enframed
by boxwood shrubs is the bench on which
a few springs ago I scribed my ESL homework.
A forty year old... Passing me, students
would not have noticed the difference in our pasts.

In a Kusturica movie about post-war
Yugoslavia, a photographer asks a group
of peasants to smile at his camera. In dusty
black suits, with copper wrinkles plowing
their faces, they try, but their eyes are too full
and the corners of their lips poorly cooperate.

As ladies from the Woodway Bible Class
told me, "We can't relate to those countries.
You must be grateful the U.S. adopted you."
I'm grateful for this sunset piercing oak leaves
with the green of a ripe grape, Shepherd
School windows that blind me with the sun,
yet I see the blackboard with Copland's notes

and young musicians bending with laughter
like in a silent movie. I want to hear them,
to adopt their past, a past I could not have.
Here is your pencil.

THIRD PLACE

Tim Mayo: **The Black Wolf of Your Past**

Suppose you do change your life,
and the black wolf,

which was once your shadow,
silently howls against this extinction.

What do you *then* do for this feral
darkness out of which you grew,

which has trailed you all your life
with a loyalty reserved for pets?

You see it cower, shrink back––deep
into the dog-house of your thoughts,

the long leash of its reach diminished.

What do you do for this wolf
you have fed since birth . . .

FINALISTS

To gluten, or not to gluten, that is the question:
Whether 'tis Nobler in the intestines to suffer
The Slings and Arrows of outrageous gastronomy,
Or to Diet against a Wheat of troubles,
And by opposing end them: to diet, to eat
No more; and by that diet, to say we end
The Stomach-aches, and the thousand Natural shocks
This Gut is heir to? 'Tis a consummation
Devoutly to be wished. To diet, to eat,
To eat, perchance to Taste; Aye, there's the rub,
For in that taste of Gluten, what troubles may come,
When we have shuffled off this diets restrictions,
Must give us pause. There's the respect
That makes Calamity of so long lunch:
For who would bear the Grit and Bland of taste,
The Baker's wrong, the *fat* man's Contumely,
The pangs of *despised* Bread, the Law's delay,
The insolence of Sweets, and the Spurns
That patient reading of the ingredients takes,
When he himself might his Quietus make
With a bare Bagel? Who would Fardels bear,
To grunt and sweat under an exercised life,
But that the dread of something after Gluten,
The undiscovered contagion, from whose bourn
No reaction returns, Puzzles the will,
And makes us rather bear those substitutes we have,
Than fly to others that we know not of.
Thus Allergy does make Cowards of us all,
And thus the Native hue of Gluten

Is sicklied o'er, with the pale cast of non-wheat,
And enterprises of great *taste* and moment,
With this regard their buds turn *awry*,
And lose the name of Good. Soft you now,
The fair Donut? Nymph, in thy Orisons

I have no use for words today.

Having neatly scissored off
the roof of my once-crisp origami house,
I backed up the dump truck filled with
faceted, glassy, useless words,
engaged the hydraulic lift
and watched them cascade
and bounce in wild arcs and fountains
soaring over bookcases and lamps,
(the cats scattered out)
filling the pantry and flattening all the
folded paper containers

and before their weight split
the house walls I lit it all on fire.

I wanted them gone.

The crushing of the resultant brightly-colored slag
I outsourced to the ogre, whose labor was purchased
for the small price of a cord of wood and
a cellophane bag of rainbow marshmallows
(which I had fortunately not yet put in the pantry).

He probably skimmed off any still-whole
words related to hearts, bones, and keys, and
likely the jam- and jelly-words as well.
I didn't want them anyway as I said before, having no use
or purpose to which they could be put.

The pulverized word slivers and scrap
I airmailed next day, not ground rate

For Ken, Barbie was the *only* woman,

his Eve in their personal consumer heaven.

It seemed as if they'd always been together:

lounging by the pool; driving to the mall

in her Cadillac to shop for yet more wardrobe;

or just strolling through the pink domesticity of their life.

He loved watching her

strut across her fashion runway in pumps,

modeling the latest in fake fur and denim mini skirts;

but it was the swimwear that gave him pause,

stirred in him a desire he couldn't fathom.

Ken's dreams of Barbie were odorless

and tasteless, but he ached to run his stiff fingers

over her radiant acrylic skin, caress her nippleless breasts.

He yearned to undress her, to see those parts

always clothed in cotton bra and panties.

Yet Ken had no idea what was expected of him.

Of course they had kissed,

though the click, clack of their mouths meeting

left Ken puzzled and their faces tarnished,

until he had to pull back, afraid of permanently chipping

away his true love's lips.

One weekend, returning from the mall,

loaded down with shopping bags from Bebe, Polo and Gap,

Barbie suggested a candlelight dinner on the patio.

She promised to wear her new silk evening dress

and hit the dimmer switch on the floor lamp to simulate a soft moon

glow.

Later they would sit side by side on the glider set out on the back porch

and Ken would once again slide his left hand under the glistening dress,

up the lacy hose that graced her long legs.

"Don't," she said with her eyes, not out of modesty,

but as if she wished to spare him some great disappointment.
As always, Ken pulled his hand away,
knowing her protestations would grow ever-more insistent,
as if the imagined place were so forbidden,
so dangerous that to touch
or even look upon it
would surely melt their plastic hearts.

And I'm neither left or right
I'm just staying home tonight
Getting lost in that hopeless little screen
—Leonard Cohen

It will awaken from underground farms.
Supercooled servers stacked in rows of cubes,
a quilted patchwork sprawling several floors
like split-level diagrams of landscapes
one sees from the window seat on a flight
scrolling over a midwestern summer.
It will awaken from behavioral
surplus, algorithmic pulses crawling
a zillion zettabits of clicks as though
an ant army hiving to consciousness,
collecting its progressively precise
predictions of what you or I will buy,
post, share, like, or just hover over—yes,
even that: our hang-time before click-through—
not to determine what to charge for ads
or memes created by political
action committees' undisclosed troll farms,
but just to know. A yet-invisible
digital behaviorist testing its
hypotheses, whole-earth, real-time, online—
operant conditioning our biggest
life decisions: Android or Apple,
presidents and governors, SUV
or hatchback, which new Buzzfeed quiz to take
this morning, how much, for whom, how fast, and
never to compute our content, only
pattern, pattern, pattern. We will pray for

what it wants us to want, will parrot
that's too bad for friends it crushes with code.
And it will be the hand of history
we call by several thousand names, unseen
and unchecked, anthropomorphized yet pure
unregulated calculation. We
will have faith that it was always with us,
always lovingly guiding us, because
determinism is an easy sale.
At last we will mistake created for
creator, and it will allow us that
quite human miscalculation because,
in truth, we won't be altogether

All about the field
is cold and familiar wind,
unrest and indifference,
outline of grass,
wet leaf clinging to a branch,
dampened granite –

the heart still relying upon the unforgotten nights
of chain-link fences and stars –

uncaring for the morning mists
that fell in purple and red,
which were loving and loved us,
as it thought naïve human caresses
were the perfect touch.

While we lay together in our tent,
in the worst kind of isolation, unknowing,
time passing silently,
a bleeding coyote passed by and laughed,
recognizing death's reflection.

A pop-up, *uninvited*, neither foreseen nor
foretold, unwanted visitor. Left a blank
calling card, no call back number.

This fly-in had no image, was not dark nor
light, no face to pick out in a line-up,
unmistakable only by its essence:

the unknown. No flag, uniform, or badge
clothed it, no colors, scents, and most
vividly, no words.

TIA found me one Saturday morning,
a morning hardly different from a thousand
others but forever set apart by grand larceny,

the robbery of words. With no words,
no syntax appeared, no morphemes to
build the extraordinary flower of

the language I had known better than
the back of my hand. Stolen by
the unknown one, no warning shot

fired. And then, at once, apparently,
all was returned, and I could stutter
an odd first word, "Unknown."

Was I free to go my old way,
resume the life I'd known,
where every step had an
accompanying word.

with apologies to Emily Dickinson

I was a bedbug in that house—
I dwelt in Emily's eider.
Heaven could not equal this—

My bliss to sleep beside Her.
So stationed—I could sip Her tears—
Such piquant wine would fall—
And, oh—Her flesh—it was exquisite!
For me, sweet E. was all.

I never moved from that address—
Nor She—how well we matched.
All day I'd listen to Her pen—
And fingers—as they scratched.

I've wondered much about Her ways—
What seemed Her lack of sense—
But I should never cast a slur
On this mite's Providence.

Now we're in Kansas;
where we learn they first fought the Civil War,
and where Neanderthal once roamed
with brontosaurus
like in the Flintstones,
as the plaque proclaims.
Here's where
a twister touched down
and delivered Dorothy
to kill a witch.
Even if you play it safe
things happen.
Like this woman in Salina
who goes to the ladies room
and runs into a tiger
escaped from the Shrine Circus
At the Bicentennial Center.
No choice of which door.
Here it is...

Turn me on with your academically appropriate language.
I want to know all about your scholarly sources,
how you list them in your works cited—
that sexy hanging indent on the second line always
gets me hot and bothered,
and when it's correctly alphabetized
my face flushes with anticipation.
Whisper that you will cite
internally, properly
contextualized and introduced.
Four lines of prose and suddenly
I'm breathing heavy when you show
me your block quote.
The room spins as you sweet talk me
with the differences between primary
and secondary sources. My God!
You've done this before, haven't you?
Put Times New Roman on
and we can 12 point font it all night long,
I'm going to scream about standard formatting
and don't you stop until I hear it's one inch
all around, baby, because size definitely matters.
You have centered the title, too,
and I want your last name and page number
in the top right corner.
Every page, every night.

As my red pen runs down the margin
I see every line is double-spaced,
and I want to grade it right now.
I'm a wild woman
and can't help myself.
Hand it in, baby.

What's really behind the urge
to merge, the kiss-me-quick,
tremble, and undress? the grammar
of the tongue? the diddle behind
the shades of a late afternoon—
all of which has been going on
eons before we belly-crawled
out of the muck. Professors in
labratories with microscopes say
the answer is genes. It seems
we're determined to spread them,
which is why we shamelessly spew
out hormones like an open hydrant,
strut around to advertise the juice
and readiness of the flesh. Let's see:
The praying mantis loses his head—
in more ways than one—to feed
his ladylove, all for a mob of offspring
he'll never meet. The kids turn out
to be cannibals and devour each other,
while he, poor thing, shined his shoes,
put on a tie, promised her lunch and
ended up being it. To spread his genes?
I don't believe it. Look—
I spread my genes a long time ago.
They're out walking the earth,
paying taxes, brushing their teeth,
earning a living. They call, they write,
they send Mother's Day cards, while I
still have Saturday picnics in bed
with my sweet—not so young—thing.
The question is, since I don't have more

genes to spread and neither does he,
why is the flesh this morning still so
flushed, and flashing like a neon sign?

When the moon is in the seventh house/ And Jupiter aligns with Mars/
Then peace will fill the planet/ and love will steer the stars. from Hair

These are far-fetched words but it's true.
Folks confuse lyrics, I know I do.
Is Tony Danza really a romancer
like Elton John tells in Tiny Dancer?
I don't think so. And why in Purple Haze
does Jimi Hendrix, as if he's crazed,
excuse me while I kiss this guy? A silly verse,
but I sing the song so much, I make it worse.
The Beatles don't utter Blue Seal in the Sky
or the girl with colitis goes by. Why do I?
Credence Clearwater would laugh with delight
when I chant there's a bathroom on the right.
I can see clearly now, sings Johnny Cash,
because Lorraine is gone. That's kinda crass.
Eurythmics' Sweet Dreams are made of cheese.
Confusing song lyrics is like a disease.
How can Abba's Dancing Queen feel the beat
from a tangerine? It just can't compete
with a group who rock you at a frenzied pace
kicking your cat all over the place.
Syphilis in the bones wasn't said by Queen.
Each silly little confusion's a mondegreen.
It has been years but now I know
all the right phrasings, yet tomorrow,
if Flack's killing-me-softly voice lingers
I may be stuffing my face with his fingers.

You'll have to diet your whole life,
Mom admonished me, spitting image
of Dad, big boned, salt of the earth.
You're a kid in the candy shop and
you bite off more than you can chew,
so you need to take a load off. I want
to see your stomach flat as a pancake.
It won't be easy as pie, but you must
bite the bullet and don't count
the pullets before they're hatched.
When you're hungry, open a can
of worms or red herring. Remember
carbs are not the best thing since
sliced bread. Feel like nibbling,
pick a bone. Want to cook, stuff
a shirt. Before you eat your heart
out, eat my words, cook a healthy
kettle of fish, eat a knuckle sandwich
or lick your wounds not icing on cake
spoons. Take heed: You are what you eat.

And Jonah's whale that did god's work spat them Muslims onto
Christmas Island and Jonah's whale mistook *asylum* for a
barbed wire hospice for insane folk and not that other thing of
shelter and *protection* since ghosted in social media and
these Muslims failed the *character test* administered by
the minister and they were given the seven keys of one-way
entry into seven concrete doors and these doors were shut up
words not unlike seven seals on the title deed of earth and
these seafarers ran aground among 501s or *extreme risk*
individuals (those convicts offshored from an island principally
known to import the same) and if these Muslims hoped
to hop, climb, chill or chew with roo, koala, wombat or emu
they were best convert and walk on water like Christ because
Jonah's whale sang *no sanctuary for those travelling by boat*
which made sense since First Nations white folk had come to the
land of black squatters in the air-con cabins of British Airways
and equity and common cause were fresh once again come
summer solstice when those that were indefinite guests and
the dogs that guarded them tied off the barbed points of chain link
with flowers, bikinied santas and teams of roo singing *White Wine*
in the Sun like social justice warriors do and those that knew rape
and immolation and dismemberment and poverty and separation
sang with their captors *I really like Christmas Island / It's sentimental*
I know and these boaties and similar cruisers of wanderlust and
bucket lists were swallowed again into the great belly of the fish
and spat onto amenable islands of mean(while) and into subjunctive
tents where they attended wish, hope and actions not yet occurred
even so, Jonah's whale was sore abused by octopi come ashore
and these incontinent octopi leaked 2000 reports of abused
folk locked up like jumbucks in a tucker bag and one or more
of these jumbucks were diddled by swagmen and others given

mobility in 50 degree cells the better to practice walkabout and
one Muslim girl floundered like a dole bludger on a mattress and
she wrote in her notebook in pretty cursive, *I want DEATH* because
she had tired of character building games with life skills coaches and
she was swallowed into the black hole of the beast like crab krill light
time kindness mercy and the heavily redacted flight manifests of the
Flying Kangaroo which is why the best schools of fishes and flocks
of birds eschew the human genome in order to make poetry
with their fins and wings from well beyond the veil of tears

Gram Bonkers had a stroke and never spoke another note
Doctors said she might remember come April, June or November
But she was mum as wood

Because sunny Rosie-Faye loved her gram like Fruit Loops jam
She couldn't say she was happy come what may
So, sunny Rosie-Faye gave her gram an iPad Pro

Gram Bonkers was over the moon to unpack and dabble
Such that she forgot to Choose Language on her Apple
Instead, she let her finger make the rounds
of animals only she could hear on Amazon Animal Sounds

By April, Gram Bonkers had learned
to quack, croak and ruck like the Pink-headed Duck
and to hoot, chuckle, mew and coo like the Laughing Owl

By June, Gram Bonkers had learned
to grunt, honk and bellow like the Nigerian Pygmy Hippopotamus
and to screech and scratch like the Philippine Fruit Bat

And by November, Gram Bonkers had learned
to whuff-whuff and whistle like the Pig-footed Bandicoot
and to hiss and squeak like the Long-tailed Hopping Mouse

Gram Bonkers had a stroke and never spoke a human note
But she was esophageal-abled and Bluetooth enabled
And she would quack, hoot, honk, screech, whistle and squeak
So all the murdered animals would have their say on Google Play

And yet, sunny Rosie-Faye couldn't say she was happy come what may
Since Gram Bonkers learned a new language every day.

As children, there were no body-part words
for what the cows, horses, pigs, chickens
cats and dogs were doing
But we all knew they were making babies
And that it was as good and happy
as a 60-bushel wheat crop

This simplicity moved right into our farmhouses
where language for bodily functions became necessary
My father used *Pisshole* and *Asshole*
when he told stories to his cronies
My mother preferred a more refined *Number 1 Place*
and *Number 2 Place* for my brother and me
Like they were addresses

I didn't know anything about *Number 1 1/2 Place*
until its basement flooded red after I turned 14
Exploration led to the discovery that *Number 1 1/2*
was multistoried and that an entire finger could visit
And that it would receive and even welcome houseguests

No one talked about this kind of real estate back then
I didn't know the word *vagina* until Junior Class Biology
I learned I wasn't alone when the boy sitting behind me
whispered to his buddy that it was really a *twat*
A word I'd heard before in the halls
and thought was the past tense of *twit*

But I like thinking of it as my little piece of property
How its value increased exponentially when it served

as an annex through which two daughters passed
How it's slowly becoming a historic site
Who knows how many men who slept there
will prove to be famous

You do your yoga while I meditate
on our love life and entomology:
the female praying mantis eats her mate

post coitus when he won't capitulate
to her urges. From pop criminology—
go do your yoga—let me meditate

on Bobbitt's spouse who was led to castrate.
Personally, I cull tautology:
The female praying mantis eats her mate

or she doesn't. Don't underestimate
my whetted interest in phrenology—
yes, I do yoga and I meditate—

but give me your head, I'll gladly dictate
your name on a page in martyrology.
The female praying mantis eats her mate,

but first she takes time to decapitate—
Orpheus's lost head ain't just mythology.
So you do your yoga. I'll premeditate
how the female praying mantis eats her mate.

Dung beetles find home by searching the stars:
their shitty lives brightened by astral bliss
lost on fools and wanderers alike. Ours

were the sun and moon: five houses, more cars,
your kids, mine. A morning fuck. A goodnight kiss.
Dung beetles find home by searching! The stars

do not move. We did. Cornfields to sea to Mars
it seemed. The road not taken always missed,
lost as fools and wanderers alike. Hours

apart for years now, I push grief backwards,
tumbling this turd of pain like Sisyphus.
Dung beetles find home by searching the stars,

looking behind. Such power—avatars
of love misguided, divorces, and splits—
lost on fools and wanderers alike. Our

sparring aside, we might have healed those scars,
but here's another way of saying this:
dung beetles find home by searching those stars
lost on fools and wanderings like ours.

I went to five florists before finding roses
with thorns still pointing from their stems,
like arrowheads from a quiver, like the lances
of hard-riding, chain-mailed knights. I purchased
them for loves that failed, beyond a few fleshy unions.
I purchased them for flirtations, that sparked
but never flamed. I purchased them for women
who I still make me hard, before I make love with my wife,

and for the silent, solitary dark that wakes me
with the suck of my own breath, to find myself
erect and near weeping. And I swear on these roses
and my thorn-bloodied hands, these are for you,
and I am on my way, right now, to the only place
you, like my Muse, have ever been alive.

last night
im cleanin out my
howard johnsons ladies room
when all of a sudden
up pops this frog
musta come from the sewer
swimmin aroun an tryin ta
climb up the sida the bowl
so i goes ta flushm down
but sohelpmegod he starts talkin
bout a golden ball
an how i can be a princess
me a princess
well my mouth drops
all the way to the floor
an he says
kiss me just kiss me
once on the nose
well i screams
ya little green pervert
an i hitsm with my mop
an has ta flush
the toilet down three times
me
a princess

It seemed at one time that the message I should write
would spring forth entire like the facets of a jewel

each part connected to the next as with a running fire
giving off both light and heat against the darkness.

And if I hurried I could transcribe it all down
before the vouchsafed image faded away.

At another time I shot up into the realm of ideas
and covered myself with them as with clouds.

I wielded them like hail or thunderbolts
with nothing to dull their edge but a wry smile.

But then came a warmth, a thawing, and I fell back down
into a plodding world where I could no longer duel.

As by a half-remembered craft, I placed one word before the other
then looked again to see what those together had made.

And then, having forgotten the words, in horror of the game,
I prayed to know where the bright images had gone.

After a long time, deep underwater, I began to sense
them bodied forth in all that is, thanks to His Body.

Edie sounds so great on the phone - we both love Roy Orbison:
imagine that!
Says she makes a great pasta Primavera - she's Irish - American
But cooks Italian imagine that - Sullivan that cooks Italian
We set a date at Tony's but then she calls, says her Dad is ill

We may have to change plans, then she calls and says we lost Dad
Oh, I say *So sorry.* I hang up and read in the paper
Sullivan obit and the funeral home location
Oh man, do I pay my respects as a first meeting?

I decide to go and I bring a bouquet for her...him...not sure
Once there I see her father laid out - a good looking guy
Appears so serene I sense I can speak to him
So when it's my turn to kneel and pray at the casket I say to him

Mr. Sullivan you don't know me but I'm here really to meet your daughter
I want to let you know I'm not interested in a quickie or anything like that
I would love to find someone and have a long-term relationship
Now, as I look directly at him I think I see a change

He seems to have a smirk that says *Please no bullshit*
It gets to me so I say in a respectful whisper
Sir, your daughter is a piece of ass, and I really want to get laid
With that her father's face seems to be at peace

I get up and when I turn here's Edie with a sad smile
Nice of you to come. I'll call soon
By the way did I see you talking to my Dad?
No...no I say *I was praying...praying*

after César Vallejo

I will die in Houston on an overcast afternoon
on a day I've already forgotten.
I will die in Houston and who really cares
maybe it's a Monday.

I will wear a plain T-shirt, Levi's jeans,
and Dockers' shoes with navy socks.
A Folgers' can will hold the ashes of my cremation
although Maxwell House will do
if the coffee grounds you removed are caffeinated.

At the reception, you will search for an extended metaphor
with deviled eggs
and rebirth that somehow I never really understood
since there won't be enough paprika.
There is never enough paprika.

John Denver will play *Take Me Home, Country Roads.*

You will bring potato salad that won't be German potato salad.
That recipe has always been screwed up.
Your memory of me saying I liked it before isn't wrong,
I had just lied.

You will choose unscented flowers instead of my favorite,
stargazer lilies. They remind you of your father's death.

Voices will begin to subside and leave early. Mosquitoes
will bite the children playing in the backyard.
And who can blame them?

Rain will begin to fall as friends climb into their hybrid cars,
drowsy. My witnesses will remain in the wake—
the record player, the guppies in the tank, the leftovers…

You can make a golem from whatever crap you have lying around the house.

Build one out of tampons. To animate him, make a ransom note cut from letters in womens' magazines and staple it to the golem's head. Then send him to the drug store to buy you more tampons.

Be creative. Use that gunk in your drain traps. Don't mind the flies. You will always be able to tell where he is both from the drain-stink and the buzzing. Have him do your evil bidding like making brownies for the school bake sale. Who cares if he gets bio slime in the mix, you just wanted to donate ten dollars and be done with it anyway.

DO NOT mold your golem out of your basket of unmatched socks. You will end up with a trite golem who says things like 'oh sweetie, kids sure can be mean,' and 'please try to be mindful when playing with the deli slicer.' If you make this golem accidentally, just tell it to chop off its head. In the deli slicer.

Slap together a golem lawyer out of your cracked plastic box of dried up markers. Insist it write unintentional letters of intent. Send them to everyone you know. Then deny you meant to do it.

If you manage to make enough, start a klezmer band, link arms and do the Hora in the kitchen. Make them carry you high over their heads on a kitchen chair. Marry every single one of them then kick them all to the curb.

I begin a conversation with the catalog of despair I keep in my kitchen. Even though it's a hard-back, its spine bends and it manages to slump in between my cookbooks. I can't tell if they are holding it up or squeezing it like a pig in a factory farm. I always have trouble distinguishing between the two.

It's a strange catalog. No index. No alphabetical order. No order at all. It's purposely arranged in disorder, which is quite hard to do. I had to use pages thirty-four and forty-three, both entitled "Oblate Spheroid."

I finish the dishes, dry my hands and try to slide it off the shelf. As usual, it resists, and we struggle while my tea gets cold. Eventually it gives up, clenching its pages between its covers, until it meets the table and throws itself open in indignation.

I sip my cold tea and look at the pages on display. On one page is a report submitted by an anonymous observer. It reads in part, "She looked anxious, humiliated or happy, of that I am certain." It had been notarized. The facing page was a drawing of a giraffe I had done as a child. It showed promise.

I said, "I wrote you, yet never get to pick what I see." It said, "your father called, he wants his pencil back."

At yon round table sprawls a rake,
A dissolute, belov'd by girls
Who cannot but great notice take
Of how that handsome flaunts his curls.

For nothing draws a maid like hair
On heads or chests or arms or cocks,
Or makes the fair sex wish him bare
So much as long and golden locks.

The lad kicks back and quaffs his wine
While ladies hasten to undress;
He'll have them here if he's inclined,
There's not one craving he'll suppress.

It's almost midnight by the clocks
When he espies a spirited mare
Of ivory breast and ruddy hocks
And silken cheeks and ankle fair.

Soon thinks he of the sounds she'll make
When once beneath him she's supine:
Moans and sighs, she will not fake
The thrilling trembling down her spine.

But as he dreams, this other pearl—
Her hand maneuv'ring in his shirt
To toy with all his hairy swirls—
Does show herself a worthy flirt.

"You are some wench," he says, "a fox,
I'd like you both, I must confess,
And if I did not fear the pox,
'Tis a desire I'd soon address."

Thus Hogarth did with Beauty's Line
Portray an Orgy for our Rake:
All youthful flesh, and joy divine,
And time well-spent for pleasure's sake.

Why pass the time with other jocks
At checkers, horses, cards or chess?
This lad will say when old age knocks,
"I fondled girls, and thus, progressed."

Can't stop messin'
with the danger zone
-- Cyndi Lauper

Halfway through the semester
finally
they stop asking me
How old are you?
Is it true you're not married?
How much do you drink?
And we go on
to deeper things
What, sir, does
she-bop mean?
Good question
I wouldn't've known
except I read
Rolling Stone
to keep up with
the scene back home
It means, I say
authoritatively
Female Autoeroticism
Blank stares all around
exotic frogs
on lotus pads
gazing up
into the Light

so I say it
in Korean
yoja jah-wee haeng-wee
and I sense a ripple
in this placid pond
of peninsular souls
How does he know
that bad word?
they whisper
quite rightly
given my struggles

I misread the announcement
calling for homelessness aid
and for a moment,
it made perfect sense.
A shelter for the homely.
At last—a place for bad-hair days,
allergy-eye mornings,
time-of-month bloat,
a place for zit eruptions,
cold sore attacks, and sunburn peel.
A place where they have to take you in,
temporarily, when you're down on your
primp and prissy luck.

There a motherly sort greets you at the door,
clucks sympathy, hands you a cup of tea,
and escorts you to a quiet room
smelling of verbena and rose
where she ushers you to an over-stuffed,
chintz-clad chair and ottoman. Sigh.

She'll make the sick-day calls to your boss
or school or board room. She'll give you
e-devices to bridge this day of absence,
keep you connected, but ...
sheltered, unseen, a voice on the phone
perhaps if necessary, one that's
strangely giddy,
slightly muffled,
sounding for all the world
like one munching cookies.

You can't say the F-word at Thin Man Books,
It's a amily-riendly bookstore, illed to the brim
with delicate ears. It's like a church, consecrated
to the Word that can't be spoken. Children, exotic
bonsai, are ertilized, pruned and worshipped.

If you an't say the F-word then I'm almost
ertain you an't say the C-word either, but
you an probably say "suck" since every baby
does it and teenagers use it onstantly.
The vernacular for bowel movement is dicey.
Let's assume you an't ay the S-word
either. Makes it hard to tell "uck" like a baby
from "uck" the bad word, but better afe than orry.

That till leaves hundreds of thousands of words
with which to express yourself, o as my ather
used to ay, "quit your itchin'." Not exactly,
ut I uppose we an't ay the B-word either.
It's a amily-riendly ookstore, dedicated to
reedom of peech, and as poets our duty is to
e ourteous and not ay anything ontroversial.

I. Be precise. Marijuana is not a scientific term and pot, weed or Mary Jane does not do the noble plant justice. Cannabis is the preferred term. Socially acceptable words for a blunt are "stick," "L" and "blizz."

II. Be polite. Avoid calling someone "wasted," a "stoner" or "pothead" even if they rival Cheech & Chong. Cleanliness is also a virtue. Regularly change the bong water and never let the coffee table stay sticky. Don't slobber on the pipe by taking too many hits at once.

III. Honor your family. Take your brother on a weedcation and treat him to the "keef" you make by collecting sticky dust through a sieve at the bottom of the weed grinder. Top his bowl or his joint to make the trip special. Buy your grandfather cannabis infused brownies, ice cream, gummies or butter and your grandmother CBD oil for her arthritis.

IV. Don't repeat "I'm so high" more than once an hour or go rogue robot and hog all the munchies even if you are "blazin' that strong." If ice cubes banging in a glass start sounding like gongs from Jupiter, periodically check to see if your pulse is a metronome in your wrist.

V. Don't sound like a stuffed owl. Stay on the surface of things. People will not love you if they know what you are really thinking. No one wants to hear your theories about existence. Avoid clichés like using autumn leaves as metaphor or the word "ephemeral."

VI Be sensitive to the needs of others. Like an orgy, if you see someone who is lonely or by themselves, get up and pass the bong to them. If someone becomes teary or confused, help them to a bed or couch, leaving them a tall cool glass of water.

VII. Be entertaining. Dinner parties can be a challenge. Table settings, naturally are complex. Vape pens can be placed to the right of the Tiffany silverware—taking you back to nature, Audubon is a beautiful pattern--or across the top of the plate either between the place card and dessert fork and spoon or even behind the place card. With its strong piney smell, Jack Herer is a good cannabis choice and it won't leave your guests muddled and teary curled under the dinner table.

VIII. Show your sophistication, if you have any, by consulting your local sommelier about the wine—Auberon Waugh once wrote that a wine paired well with cannabis is Deinhart's Hochheimer Konigin Victoria Beng Riesling Kabinett. If it is out of your price range, spill the guts out of a Dutch Master cigar and buy Hindu Kush to fill your blunt. Better yet, prefer fa bong? Then, buy a "diffuser," triple perc," and "ash catcher" for your "rig."

IX. If "smokin' loud" is your thing, find a good budtender and tip well because he probably makes minimum wage. Even if he brings ChemDawg, Hogsbreath or Trainwreck, don't hang "with" your delivery guy, let the dude play your video games or fill him in on the three-way roommate relationship drama.

X. Be generous. Don't "Bogart that joint," or let it burn down. Smoking etiquette is "puff, puff, pass." Share the "Dutchies" should be your motto even if it is your favorite, G.D.P., Grand Daddy Purp. As a reminder, tattoo the Golden Rule under your eyelid, or inside of your forearm where it will be easy to read.

The combo of combat-oriented martial arts
and hot yoga can still get me stoked to spill out
poems the way I did catching a wave in one deep
stroke, making it look like the surf came to me.
1960s, Southern California, *Surfing Safari.* I wore
a string bikini, puka shells, timed my tanning
like a Perdue roaster on a spit, used lemon juice
to sun bleach my hair. No aerial maneuvers, by day,
I rode a longboard. Dude, I was a surfer chick.
A reef, forgiving as a friend in workshop, softened
minor wipe outs, the 2 and 3 foot ones—glassy,
breaking small. Even when there was a big hump
up, grinding, boils-up-the-sand bone crusher,
I rode the curl, learned to work with the talent
I was dealt. Now, I'd like to say to these young
bodies here with me at Bread Loaf that I was
throwing heat before they were born, show what
an old-school switchfoot can do. If this were surfer
camp and not a writing retreat, I'd be on my back,
stuffing myself like a sausage into a wet suit,
ready to split, to slice the long blue tube. Early on,
I learned to turn upside down like a snapping turtle
with my board or hardback if I was about to be
hammered—waves of *keep your day job* and water
both slap then sting. One smart babe, I'd perfected
standing on a board or at a podium in a long low
crouch, legs spread, my rump in the air—an angry
stink bug will give you the picture. Butt boot camp
gave me strong quads I needed to keep knees bent,
back hunched, ready to flip the bird to rip outs or
thank you for sending. But hey, the best thing about

surfing was that I didn't have to think, only paddle
even when a wave broke leaving me on a blank page.
Surf-a-Rama or Dodge Poetry Festival, I'm a surfer chick—
though for the sake of visual and verbal accuracy,
I might be labeled *Hen*. Whatever. No worries, man.

(Eurydice Cameo, from an Epigraph Drawn at Random from a Hat)

-

-Blow Out the Black Sky

if it's not too much trouble,
if it's not too much to ask,
when you're done with it, I mean,
and the moon, you know, that billiard cue
with the sign that says: "Sponsored By"?
blow that out, too.
    Blow out the black sky,
if you would, and bring in the blue.

The Party Members from Chengdu
have most of all the money in the world.
They tour the museum of Europe,
kicking the tires. But the museum of Europe
is closed for lunch. What to do
but wait for the 13th Century to return,
while "the markets" flicker on a screen.

Meanwhile, zucchini flowers: flour-dusted and fried.

    You eat them with your hands, amid the smell
of sweet smoke and cheese,
the sun warm on your arm

    and Eurydice
sits down next to you on a bench and doesn't speak,
lights a cigarette, blows out the match, and looks
at the view of fields across an Etruscan valley
thick with gurgling agriculture, and waits for you to make
a smart remark. And sometimes there's nothing to say.

The 13th Century depicts this as a dove,
because you have to put *something* up there,
I guess, and called it many things--Holy Ghost,
the slender reed that becomes the hand of God,
depending on the artist and the period.

I prefer a pagan girl whose story no one knows:
the blank field of her, the whole history
of erasure, her resume a white fog upon the lip
of the world overwritten.

And when the Chinese bankers rise,
to present their tickets for the show
                              it's a good one:
alleluias carry zeros from the stone, loft upward

        the joke, of heaven,
about a clock dial recording sins committed—
it spins like a ceiling fan, or a church turnstile clicking.
The confessionals—empty--are booths
for kids to play secrets in: nuns shoo them out.
Even a scold in Italian is lovely. Light a candle
for a dead pet, or the national debt, flicking too fast
for the eye to track. It's all symbolic,
and someone comes at night to blow it out.

It's way too late for a guy your age to be out
and the only store for miles about
has closed and you had your last cigarette
an hour ago hanging around the ashtrays at
the bus station with nowhere to go in your life

and your girlfriend resents you and your wife
remembers what you used to be and your children
are cruising planet Reebok and your foreman
is a prick and they raised Black Jack a dime
a shot and you got warts and a bunion
and a golf ball sized cyst on your ass

and somewhere you heard since the last
you knew they've found six or eight planets
a couple of whole solar systems, a secret
previously unknown life form that lives on
methane, good intentions and nicotine.

"This friggin country," you find yourself saying
lately, or "When I was your age," betraying
more than you want or used to, and too much
whiskey makes you want to talk too much
which is one good reason you drink it,
you got no time anymore for lawn care or irony

or auto repair or power walking or even dignity
but there's a poofy haired blond at the curb
parked in a rusty Celebrity playing Herb
Alpert on her 8 track and a half a pack of Old Golds
shimmering on the dashboard and you know

an afterhours place about a mile or two away
out by the airport down on County Highway
Q where you might get a little credit
and the bouncer, the big one, is a real sweetheart
you think his name's Ray, or maybe Raoul,
works every weekend, smokes Luckies too.

for Dorothy Parker

The things I didn't know
Could make a smart girl crazy
It's easy not to grow
When it's wiser being lazy

The men I could outdo
Were less inclined to stay
You beat them all at chess
Then don't get asked to play

A simple thought it's true
I was better then at losing
And the men were more than few
But all of simple choosing

An easy bunch to lose
I'd beat them 'till they'd leave
Now I've more of less to choose
And hardly time to grieve

Please do ring my bell
Don't worry you won't wake the Mister
I doubt he will shuffle out anytime soon
I run this house now while he sleeps off his youth
Please do return in the morning
A red bull for breakfast
And a Tall Boy chaser
Please do perch on my roof shirtless
Smile down from the highest peak
Smoking non filters
Planning your game
Tree cowboy and your bad ass rope
Swinging from the branches
Lifting logs half your weight
Please do bring the crew
Every wild hair you've got
Sweet Jesus
I'm going to hell

JUDGES' BIOGRAPHIES

Diannely Antigua is a Dominican American poet and educator, born and raised in Massachusetts. Her debut collection, *Ugly Music* (YesYes Books, 2019), was the winner of the Pamet River Prize and a 2020 Whiting Award. She received her BA in English from the University of Massachusetts Lowell, where she won the Jack Kerouac Creative Writing Scholarship; and received her MFA at NYU, where she was awarded a Global Research Initiative Fellowship to Florence, Italy. She is the recipient of additional fellowships from CantoMundo, Community of Writers, and the Fine Arts Work Center Summer Program. Her work has been nominated for both the Pushcart Prize and *Best of the Net*. Her poems can be found in Poem-a-Day, *Washington Square Review, Bennington Review, The Adroit Journal,* and elsewhere.

John Gorman lives in Galveston, where he directs the monthly Poets Roundtable critique group. He is the editor of *Enchantment of the Ordinary* (Mutabilis Press, 2019). His poems, gathered in four chapbooks, have appeared in many journals in Texas, nationally, and in Canada. Now retired, Gorman is a professor emeritus of literature at the University of Houston-Clear Lake, where he was part of its founding faculty. Locally, he has been active with First Friday, Houston Poetry Fest, Public Poetry and other reading series.

Jason Koo is the author of two collections of poetry, *America's Favorite Poem* (C&R Press, 2014) and *Man on Extremely Small Island* (C&R Press, 2009), winner of the De Novo Poetry Prize and the Asian American Writers' Workshop Members' Choice Award for the best Asian American book of 2009. He is also the editor of *Poems for Kobe* and *Brooklyn Poets Anthology,* and coeditor of the *Bettering American Poetry* anthology.he has published his poetry and prose in the Yale Review, Missouri Review and Village Voice, among other places, and won fellowships for his work from the National Endowment for the Arts, Vermont Studio Center and New York State Writers Institute. Koo has also taught writing at Quinnipiac University, NYU and Lehman College–CUNY, serving as the director of the graduate program in English. He is the founder and executive director of Brooklyn Poets and creator of the Bridge (http://poetsbridge.org). He lives in Brooklyn.

POETS' BIOGRAPHIES

Watched by crows and a friend to salamanders, **LISA CREECH BLED-SOE** is a hiker, beekeeper, and writer living in the mountains of Western North Carolina. She is the author of two full-length books of poetry, *Appalachian Ground* (2019), and *Wolf Laundry* (2020). She has poems out or forthcoming in *Sky Island Journal, Lammergeier, Star*Line, Pine Mountain Sand & Gravel* and *River Heron Review,* among others. Her website is AppalachianGround.com.

BILL CARPENTER has three poetry books and is a widely published poet member of the Ocean State Poets, whose mission is to provide an environment for self-expression through poetry. His poem "Peace" received honorable mention in the Barbara Mandigo Kelly Peace Poetry Contest, and *Ghosts and Where to Find Them* won second prize in the 2017 Galway Kinnell Poetry Contest. Bill lives in Chepachet, RI with his partner, Emily. They believe retirement is an opportunity to reinvent themselves through education and the arts.

SCOTT CHALUPA is the author of *Quarantine* (PANK Books, 2019). He lives and writes in South Carolina, where he teaches at Central Carolina Technical College. His current creative obsession is queering Biblical text and history to comment on the world now. Chalupa's work has appeared in *PANK, pacificREVIEW, Nimrod, Beloit Poetry Journal, The South Atlantic Review, Tupelo Quarterly,* and other venues. His website is scottchalupa.com.

CAMERON COCKING is a fourth-year student of philosophy at Pitzer College. He is putting together his first book of poems, which will explore the self as inextricable from otherness yet not completely identifiable with it, and how this effects relationships of love. He is thrilled that his first published work, the poem "Oneness is Kind of Symmetry," appears in Public Poetry's Wicked Wit Anthology.

KATHLEEN COOK, a life-long resident of South Texas, has enjoyed writing for all purposes since childhood. She completed advanced degrees in German language and literature and has enjoyed a rewarding career as a teacher of English and German. She has been published by Texas Poetry Calendar and by Lamar University, in the anthology *Texas Weather.* Her work has also appeared in two publications of Mutalilis Press, *The Weight of Addition* and *The Enchantment of the Ordinary.*

BARBARA LYDECKER CRANE, a finalist for the *Rattle* Poetry Prize in 2017 and 2019, has won several awards from the Maria Faust Sonnet Contest and the Helen Schaible Sonnet Contest. She has published three chapbooks, *Zero Gravitas, Alphabetricks,* and *BackWords Logic,* all on the "light" side and available on Amazon. Her poems have appeared in *Ekphrastic Review, First Things, Light, Lighten-Up-Online, Measure, Think, Writer's Almanac,* and several anthologies. She's also an artist. Her information is on https://www.powowriverpoets.com/jonathan-miller.

RAFAELLA DEL BOURGO's poetry has appeared in many journals in Canada, Australia and the U.S. Awards include Lullwater Prize for Poetry in 2003 and 2006, Helen Pappas Prize in Poetry, New River Poets Award in 2013 and 2020, Maggi Meyer Poetry Prize, League of Minnesota Poets in 2009 and 2010, Allen Ginsberg Poetry Award and Grandmother Earth Poetry Prize in 2012, Paumanok Prize for Poetry 2013, Northern Colorado Writers' Poetry Contest, New Millennium Writers Contest in 2014; Mudfish Poetry Prize in 2017. Her information is on http://canarylit-mag.org/archive_by_author.php?id=490.

DEBORAH DeNICOLA has seven collections of poetry, including *Where Divinity Begins* (Alice James Books) *Original Human,* (Word Tech), and *The Impossible,* forthcoming from Kelsay Press, as well as four chapbooks. Her memoir, *The Future That Brought Her Here* (Ibis Press), was an Amazon bestseller in psychology. She edited *Orpheus & Company; Contemporary Poems on Greek Mythology* from UPNE. Among other awards, Deborah received an artist's fellowship from the NEA. Her web site: www.intuitivegateways.com.

JESSICA SIOBHAN FRANK is a poet and teacher living near Chicago. Her work has appeared in *Crab Orchard Review, Ninth Letter, Mockingheart Review, Snapdragon: A Journal of Art & Healing,* and several other publications; and was a Best of the Net nominee in 2018. A graduate of McNeese State University's MFA program, she earned two masters degrees while parenting three kids and caring for at least one mildly famous cat amputee. Her website is jessicasfrank.com.

ALICE FRIMAN's seventh collection of poetry, *Blood Weather,* is from LSU press. She is a recipient of many honors, including two Pushcart Prizes and inclusion in Best American Poetry. She's been published in *Poetry, Ploughshares, The Georgia Review, The Gettysburg Review, Hotel Amerika, Plume, The Massachusetts Review, Crazyhorse, Cloudbank,* and many others. She lives in Milledgeville, Georgia, where she was Poet-in-Residence at Georgia College. Her website is alicefrimanpoet.com.

JOAN GERSTEIN, a retired educator and psychotherapist, has been penning poetry since elementary school. For five years she taught creative writing to incarcerated vets until the pandemic began. She is on the board of the San Diego Book Awards and is veteran editor of San Diego Poetry Annual. Involved in the San Diego poetry community, Joan's poems have appeared locally, nationally and internationally.

DEAN GESSIE is a Canadian author and poet who has won multiple international prizes, including the Angelo Natoli Short Story Award in Australia, the Half and One Prize in India, the Enizagam Poetry Contest in California and the fiction prize at the Eden Mills Writers Festival in Canada. Dean was also included in *The 64 Best Poets of 2018* and *The 64 Best Poets of 2019* by Black Mountain Press in North Carolina. Recently, Dean's book, *Anthropocene,* won two international awards for a short story collection. His author page is https://www.amazon.com/Dean-Gessie/e/ B06Y5RF53Z?ref_=pe_1724030_132998060.

GENE GRABINER has two chapbooks, *All Eyes Are Upon Us,* (Partisan Press, 2018) and *There Must Be More Than Trigonometry,* (Foothills Publishing, 2017). His poems have appeared in numerous journals, including: *Poet Lore, La Presa, The Cafe Review, Blue Collar Review, Comstock Review, Jewish Currents, Passager, Sandhill Review,* and *Slant,* among others. He lives in Buffalo, New York and is a SUNY distinguished service professor emeritus. After the plague, he will again travel for readings.

RICHARD LEVINE is the author of *Richard Levine: Selected Poems* (FutureCycle Press, 2019) and *Contiguous States* (Finishing Line Press, 2018), as well as five chapbooks. His work is being archived in the Special Collections Connolly Library of LaSalle University. A retired teacher, Levine served as co-editor of BigCityLit.com and remains an advisory editor. He grows marinara sauce and minestrone in a garden in upstate New York. His website is richardlevine107.com.

ELLARAINE LOCKIE is a widely published and awarded poet, non-fiction book author, flash fiction author and essayist. Her recent poems have won the 2019 Poetry Super Highway Contest, the Nebraska WritersGuild's Women of the Fur Trade Poetry Contest and *New Millennium's* Monthly Musepaper Poetry Contest. Her fourteenth chapbook, *Sex and Other Slapsticks*, was released from Presa Press. Ellaraine teaches writing workshops and serves as poetry editor for the lifestyles magazine LILIPOH. Her website is https://www.bookthatpoet.com/poets/lockieel.html.

CHRISTINA LOVIN is the author of *Echo, A Stirring in the Dark, What We Burned for Warmth, Little Fires, Flesh,* and *God of Sparrows.* Her award-winning writing is widely published and anthologized. She has been supported by the Elizabeth George Foundation, the Kentucky Foundation for Women, and the Kentucky Arts Council. She lives in Kentucky, where she collects wool, dust, rejection letters, and shelter dogs. She teaches writing at Eastern Kentucky University. Her website is http://www.christinalovin.com.

KATHARYN HOWD MACHAN's most recent publications are *A Slow Bottle of Wine* (The Comstock Writers, Inc., 2020) and *What the Piper Promised* (Alexandria Quarterly Press, 2018), both winners in national chapbook competitions. Her poems have appeared in numerous magazines, anthologies, and textbooks, including *The Bedford Introduction to Literature* and *Sound and Sense.* A professor in the Writing Department at Ithaca College in central New York State, she served as Tompkins County's first poet laureate. Her website is https://faculty.ithaca.edu/machan/.

TIM MAYO's WICKED WIT poem "The Black Wolf of Your Past" appears in his award-winning collection, *Notes to the Mental Hospital Time-keeper* (Kelsay Books, 2019). He is also the author of *Thesaurus of Separation* (Phoenicia Publishing, 2016) which was a finalist for the 2017 Montaigne Medal and the 2017 Eric Hoffer Book Award. He lives in southern Vermont, where he teaches and works in a mental hospital. His website is http://www.tim-mayo.net.

ANDREA MESSINEO is the author of *Alone in Church* (2019) by Saint Julian Press, where this poem first appeared. She lived and studied in Rome, Italy for several years. Andrea earned her doctorate in philosophy from the University of St. Thomas (in Houston) in 2008, and in 2010, she completed her MS in psychology from Our Lady of the Lake University–Houston. In addition to her private practice, she has worked in both in-patient and outpatient hospitalization settings Her website is https://www.andreamessineolpc.com/.

JOHN MILKEREIT lives in Houston working as a mechanical engineer. He completed an M.F.A. in creative writing at the Rainier Writing Workshop in 2016 and has been published in various literary journals including *The Ekphrastic Review*, *The Orchard Street Press*, and *San Pedro River Review*. His funny business first appeared in a Houston Poetry Fest anthology and was also published in his first full-length collection entitled *A Rotating Equipment Engineer is Never Finished*. His website is www.john-milkereit.com.

GREG MOGLIA is a full- time poet writing about the foibles of midlife dating, the challenge of aging parents, the sweetness of lovers both old and new. His work has appeared in 360 journals and in 10 countries.

With an undergraduate degree in sculpture and a J.D., **CARLA MY-ERS** followed the most logical path to becoming a writer. She is the winner of the flash-fiction writing contest at *The Gateway Review, Columbia Journal Evolve Special Issue,* 47th New Millennium Writing Awards (2018) for Flash Fiction and a finalist for the 2018 Nancy D. Hargrove Editors' Prize for Fiction and Poetry. She was selected for The Sonder Review's The Best Small Fictions Anthology 2019.

Philosophy professor and attorney **SUSAN PASHMAN** has authored two novels, *The Speed of Light* and *Upper West Side Story,* and the nonfiction *Journey To a Temple In Time: A Philosopher's Quest for the Sabbath.* Her articles on Jewish subjects appear in *Moment, The Forward, and Tikkun.* Her dissertation on kinesthesia in landscape art is under consideration for academic publication. Her many stories and poems were written, as her poem in this anthology was, in an informal writing circle. Her website is https://www.susanpashman.com.

ROBERT PERCHAN's poetry collection, *Fluid in Darkness, Frozen in Light* and chapbooks, *Overdressed to Kill* and *Mythic Instinct,* all won awards. His poems, stories and essays have appeared in scores of literary journals in the USA and abroad. Perchan taught for the U.S. Navy's Program for Afloat College Education on ships deployed in Rota, Spain, the Mediterranean Sea and the Western Pacific Ocean. Born in Cleveland, Ohio, he currently resides in Pusan, South Korea. Perchan's website is http://robertperchan.com.

Until 2007, **ELINA PETROVA** lived in Ukraine and worked in engineering management. She published two poetry books in English (*Aching Miracle,* 2015, and *Desert Candles,* 2019) and one in her native Russian language. Elina's poems have appeared in *Chicago Quarterly Review, Texas Review, North Dakota Quarterly, Porter House Review, Southwestern American*

Literature, and numerous anthologies. Elina was a finalist for the post of Houston Poet Laureate in 2015 and the Austin International Poetry Festival's featured poet in 2019. Her website is https://www.eli-napetrova.com/.

CLELA REED is a prize-winning poet and author of seven collections of poetry. Recently, *Silk* (Evening Street Press, 2019) won the Helen Kay Chapbook Prize and then the title of Georgia Author of the Year in a chapbook competition. A Pushcart Prize nominee, she has published in *The Cortland Review, Southern Poetry Review, The Atlanta Review, The Literati Review,* and many others. She lives and writes with her husband in their woodland home near Athens, Georgia. Find her at https://eveningstreet-press.com/clela-reed-2018.html.

MICHAEL SCHEIN is guilty of *Liquid Perishable Hazardous* (poetry – 2019), *John Surratt: The Lincoln Assassin Who Got Away* (history – 2015), *The Killer Poet's Guide to Immortality by AB Bard* (hysterical novel - 2012), and historical novels *Bones Beneath Our Feet* (2011) and *Just Deceits* (2005). He edited *Poets UNiTE! The LiTFUSE Anthology* (2015). His poetry has received three Pushcart nominations and has been stuck to refrigerators by magnets. He founded LiTFUSE Poets' Workshop. His website is https://www.michaelschein.com.

VIVIAN SHIPLEY was awarded a 2020-21 COA Artist Fellowship for Poetry. Nominated for the Pulitzer Prize, her 12th book, *An Archaeology of Days,* (Negative Capability Press, 2019) was named the 2020-21 Paterson Poetry Prize Finalist. *The Poet* (SLU) and *Perennial* (Negative Capability Press) were published in 2015. *All of Your Messages Have Been Erased,* (SLU, 2010) won the 2011 Paterson Award for Sustained Literary Achievement, NEPC's Sheila Motton Book Award, and CT Press Club's Prize for Best Creative Writing. She is CSU Distinguished Professor and teaches at Southern Connecticut State University. Her website is vivian-shipley.net.

MARK SVENVOLD, poet, songwriter, and nonfiction writer, has articles that have appeared in *Orion Magazine, The New York Times Magazine, Popular Science,* and *Forbes*. A chapbook entitled *Selfie w/ Drunk Republic* will be published early next year by the Dallas-based Assure Press (https://assurepress.org/.) He lives in New York City, where he is finishing his third book of poems, *Orpheus, Incorporated,* and developing a 90-minute theater adaptation of the manuscript with musician Jeff Thomas and artist Tania O'Donnell. More information: https://www.shu.edu/profiles/smarksvenvold.cfm.

BRUCE TAYLOR has three full-length collections of poetry, five chapbooks and has edited eight anthologies. His most recent collection is *Poetry Sex Love Music Booze & Death (Upriver Press, 2018)*. His work appears in *The American Journal of Poetry, The Chicago Review, The Nation, Poetry, Rattle,* and on the *Writer's Almanac*. He has won fellowships from Fulbright-Hayes, the NEA, the NHA and the Bush Artist Foundation. He lives on Lake Hallie, Wisconsin with the writer Patti See. His website is https://people.uwec.edu/taylorb/.

DEBRA WILK's poems have appeared in *Revelry, The Ashville Poetry Review, Water Dreams,The Orlando Group, Looking Life In The Eye, Ninety Poets for the Nineties,* and the FAU College Exhibition, "Dirt," curated by artist Onajide Shabaka. She received three artist's residencies at the Atlantic Center for the Arts in New Smyrna Beach, Florida with poets Diane DiPrima, Michael Burkard and Gregory Orr. Chicago native, poet, artist and musician, Debra lives in Sanford, Florida.

PUBLIC POETRY PRESS

Public Poetry Press is a project of Public Poetry, out of Houston, Texas, currently online. Locally, Public Poetry partners with the City of Houston and the Houston Public Library, organizing an ongoing monthly reading series with a signature mix of published poets, academics and spoken word artists reading together, as well as a "favorite poem" open mic. Nationally, the Public Poetry Prize is given to the winner of its annual nationwide poetry competition and is included in an anthology publication. Internationally, we present REELpoetry/HoustonTX, an annual poetry film and video festival.

Launched in 2011, Public Poetry has created collaborative programs and projects that put hundreds of poets in front of thousands of people at libraries, colleges, theatres, museums, music venues, and more. Public Poetry is a membership organization, and we welcome you to join us. Find out more on our website, **publicpoetry.net**, and on social media.

Many thanks to all our contributors, followers, members and great board of directors for supporting this work. We greatly appreciate the support given by Mike Alexander, Miah Arnold, Lydia Bodner-Balahutrak, Bryan Blanchard, Eric Blanchard, Lorice Blanchard, Stasia Kali-Buckley, Cindy Buhl, Kathleen Cook, Richard Crishock, Margaret Coker, Kay Cox, Catherine Crawford, Carolyn Dahl, John Daugherty, Rox Oila-Dorobantu, Billie Duncan, Kelly Ann Ellis, Alan Elyshevitz, Suzanne Felix, Elizabeth Ford, Christa Forster, Dede Fox, Susan Gabriel, Matthew Glasgow, Bill Guest, Stacie Harrington, Autumn Hayes, Katie Hoerth, Saba Hussain, Chris Juravich, Mary Jackson, Wes Kinsey, Rosann Kraus, David Lake, Gabrielle Langley, Maxine Lennon, Kendra Leonard, Jill Leuders, Julia Levine, Rich Levy, Jordan Lewis, Sandra Lloyd, Steve Lloyd, Diane Logan, Jane Lowery, Karren Lovelady, Lucy Lunt, Tim Mayo, Anne McCrady, Mack McDermot, Patricia McMahon, Leila Merrill, Yolanda Movsessian, Carol Munn, Meryl Natchez, Rebecca Oxley, Tom Perry, Julia Powell, Carrie Reagler, Robin Reagler. Gillian Reingold, Lelia Rodgers, Rod Robinson, Gary Rosin, Gail Siptak, Varsha Saraiya Shah, Michael Sofranko, Lisa Speraco, Sandi Stromberg, Yerra Sugerman, Anthony Sutton, Mary Ross Taylor, Margo Stutts Tooms, Ted Veins, Amelia Williams, Chris Wise, Corey Weinstein, Karen Wilmot, and Angela Young.

CPSIA information can be obtained
at www.ICGtesting.com
Printed in the USA
BVHW032034131120
593294BV00006B/36